How do we stop climate change?

Written by Tom Jackson

Illustrated by Dragan Kordić

Foreword by Dr. Marianna Linz, Harvard University

EARTHAWARE
KIDS

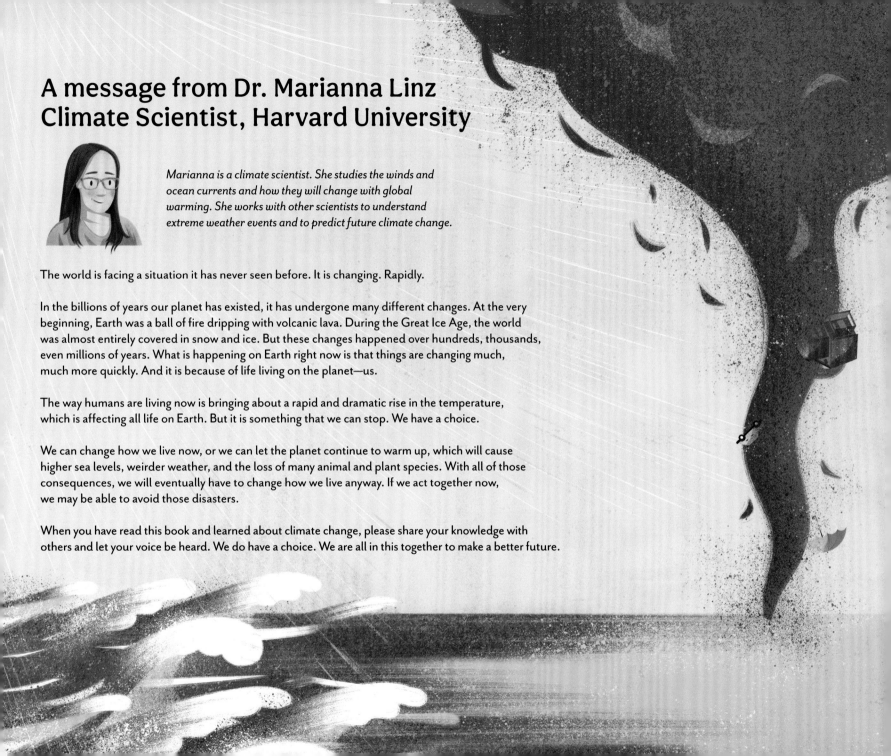

A message from Dr. Marianna Linz
Climate Scientist, Harvard University

Marianna is a climate scientist. She studies the winds and ocean currents and how they will change with global warming. She works with other scientists to understand extreme weather events and to predict future climate change.

The world is facing a situation it has never seen before. It is changing. Rapidly.

In the billions of years our planet has existed, it has undergone many different changes. At the very beginning, Earth was a ball of fire dripping with volcanic lava. During the Great Ice Age, the world was almost entirely covered in snow and ice. But these changes happened over hundreds, thousands, even millions of years. What is happening on Earth right now is that things are changing much, much more quickly. And it is because of life living on the planet—us.

The way humans are living now is bringing about a rapid and dramatic rise in the temperature, which is affecting all life on Earth. But it is something that we can stop. We have a choice.

We can change how we live now, or we can let the planet continue to warm up, which will cause higher sea levels, weirder weather, and the loss of many animal and plant species. With all of those consequences, we will eventually have to change how we live anyway. If we act together now, we may be able to avoid those disasters.

When you have read this book and learned about climate change, please share your knowledge with others and let your voice be heard. We do have a choice. We are all in this together to make a better future.

Contents

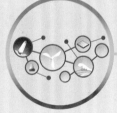

Mind mapping

The reason this book is called Mind Mappers is because it is organized like a mind map. A mind map is a picture diagram that connects lots of different ideas. It is a very useful way to make complicated topics easy to understand. The mind map on this page looks at the question that is the title of this book–"How do we stop climate change?" It divides the subject into the eight further questions, which are at the beginning of each chapter.

Follow the lines

Find the question that you would like to explore and follow the colored lines to look at the individual topics. For example, there are three main ways to stop climate change—with renewable energy, by letting nature play its part, and by reducing our carbon footprint. Keep following the lines to see how these topics subdivide.

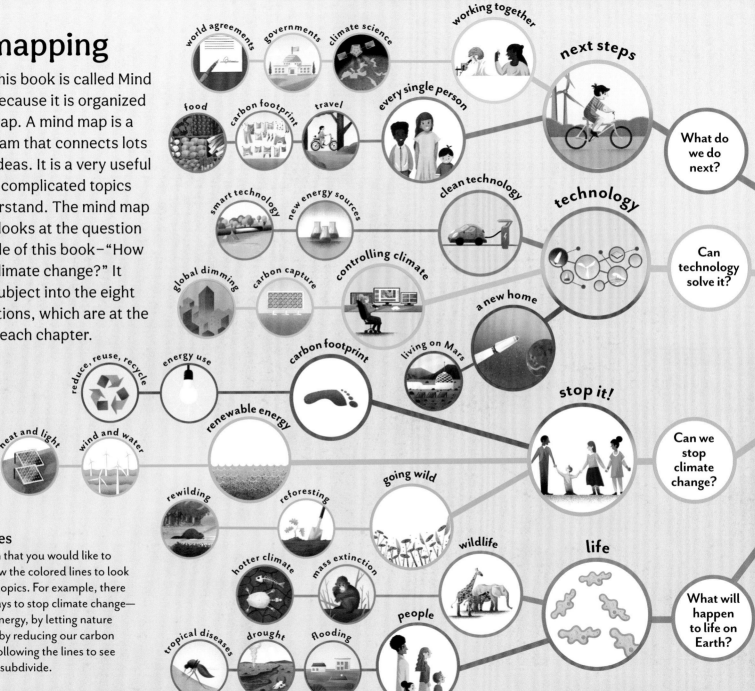

world agreements

governments

climate science

working together

next steps

What do we do next?

food

carbon footprint

travel

every single person

smart technology

new energy sources

clean technology

technology

Can technology solve it?

global dimming

carbon capture

controlling climate

a new home

living on Mars

reduce, reuse, recycle

energy use

carbon footprint

stop it!

heat and light

wind and water

renewable energy

Can we stop climate change?

rewilding

reforesting

going wild

wildlife

life

hotter climate

mass extinction

people

What will happen to life on Earth?

tropical diseases

drought

flooding

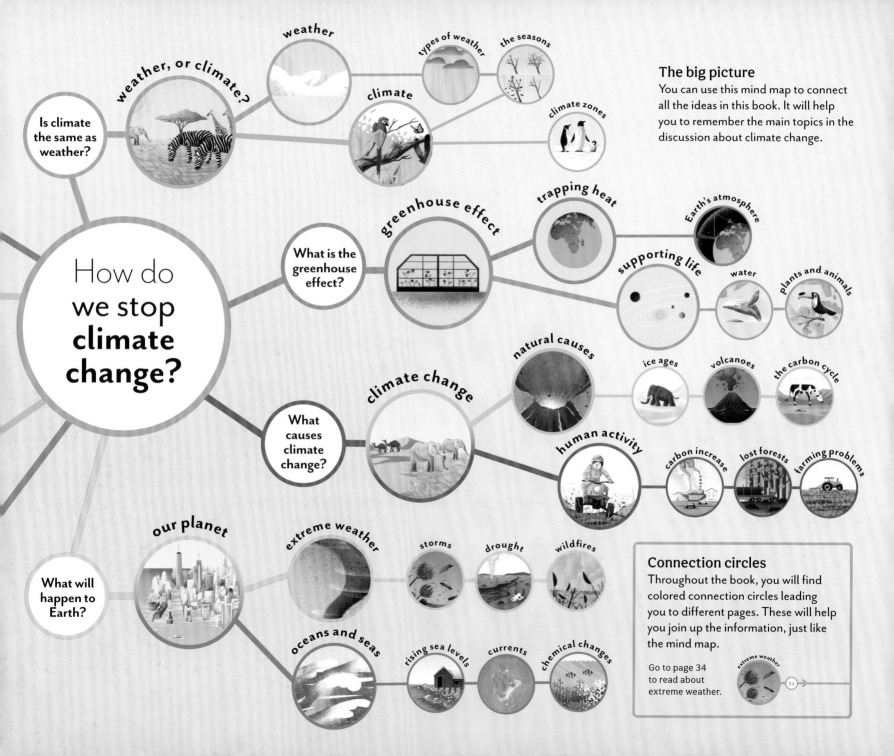

weather, or climate?

weather

types of weather

the seasons

climate

climate zones

Is climate the same as weather?

The big picture
You can use this mind map to connect all the ideas in this book. It will help you to remember the main topics in the discussion about climate change.

greenhouse effect

trapping heat

Earth's atmosphere

supporting life

water

plants and animals

What is the greenhouse effect?

How do we stop **climate change?**

climate change

natural causes

ice ages

volcanoes

the carbon cycle

What causes climate change?

human activity

carbon increase

lost forests

farming problems

our planet

extreme weather

storms

drought

wildfires

What will happen to Earth?

Connection circles
Throughout the book, you will find colored connection circles leading you to different pages. These will help you join up the information, just like the mind map.

Go to page 34 to read about extreme weather.

oceans and seas

rising sea levels

currents

chemical changes

extreme weather

34

is climate the same as weather?

Weather and climate are two separate things. Weather changes from day to day, from hour to hour. Climate changes very slowly over a period of time—months, a year, or millions of years. Today, climate change is affecting our weather. It is making it more extreme.

weather, or climate?

It may be cold and wet, or sunny and dry, bitterly cold, or stickily hot. Weather is this mixture of events that happens to us, and it changes all the time. "Climate" refers to a more gradual shift over a longer period.

weather

Weather is what is around us in the air wherever we are. It happens every day of our lives. Weather is affected by many different things, including the changing seasons.

climate

"Climate" is a description of the kinds of weather that an area gets throughout the year or longer. An area's climate is affected by the conditions in its location, or zone.

types of weather

8

the seasons

10

climate zones

12

Types of weather

Weather is what is going on outside right now. It may be sunshine, rain, snow, wind, or a storm. Many different things affect the weather, including air movement, temperature, and air pressure. Weather is not the same as climate, but climate change is making our weather more extreme.

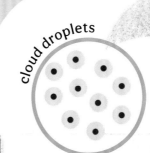

cloud droplets

Inside a cloud

Cloud droplets and ice crystals form around tiny specks of dust that are floating in the air. Billions of them make up a single fluffy cloud.

Condensation

As water vapor rises, it cools. It then condenses, turning back into water droplets and forming ice crystals. These stay in the sky as clouds.

The water cycle

Water makes weather happen. Most water is in the oceans, rivers, lakes, and ice caps. A smaller amount stays in the air all the time but is constantly being recycled in the water cycle.

Falling droplets

When the drops of water and ice crystals that make up clouds grow too big, they fall as rain or snow.

Runoff

Most rainwater runs off the land into rivers and streams, and then back into the oceans.

Evaporation

The Sun's heat warms the surface of the oceans, causing it to evaporate. The water changes into water vapor and rises into the air.

Wind

When air is warmed by the Sun, it rises. This leaves space for air from a cooler area to move in and replace it. The movement of this air creates the wind.

Hurricane superstorms

These are also called typhoons and cyclones and are the biggest storms in the world. They can grow into a wide spiral of cloud that travels very quickly.

Snow

It snows when cloud droplets are big enough and cold enough to form ice crystals that fall.

Hail

When the wind blows raindrops up high, they may freeze into hailstones. These then plummet to the ground.

extreme weather   34

Extreme weather

When there are big changes in temperature and pressure, more extreme weather occurs. These include destructive lightning storms, hurricanes, tornadoes, flooding, and droughts.

How air moves

Air is a gas. It is made up of tiny units called molecules that move in all directions. The way air moves depends on its temperature and pressure. Cold air brings high pressure, while warm air brings low pressure.

sinking cool air

air warms up and spreads out

rising warm air

cooler air moves in to replace rising air

Warm air

When air warms up, the molecules move around faster and push each other apart. The air rises.

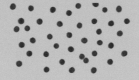

Cool air

Molecules slow down when it is cold and take up less space. The air gets denser and sinks.

High pressure

When air cools it sinks, and more air presses down on the Earth's surface.

Low pressure

When air warms it rises, so less air is pressing down on Earth's surface.

Climate connections

Climate change is creating big changes in temperature. This is causing hotter heat waves, stronger winds, and longer droughts. The warming air evaporates more water, which makes storms more extreme.

The seasons

Earth's four seasons are caused by the way that our planet moves round the Sun. As Earth travels, it spins on a slight tilt. When it leans towards the heat of the Sun, there is a warm summer. When it leans away from the Sun, there is a cold winter. Each season begins as the Earth reaches a different stage on its journey. Climate change is altering the length of our seasons.

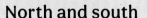

March

Winter warms into spring in the north. Autumn begins in the south.

northern spring

Equator

southern autumn

North and south

Earth is divided into two halves by an imaginary line called the Equator. When it is summer in the north, it is winter in the south, and vice versa.

June

The north tilts towards the Sun, so it is summer. But it is cold winter in the south.

northern summer

southern winter

Summer

Trees now have full green leaves. There is more light during the day for longer.

Day length

It is warm during summer because the Sun is high in the sky. It rises early and sets late. In winter, the Sun stays low in the sky all day. Sunrise is much later and sunset is earlier.

Spring

The weather starts to get warm. The trees begin to grow leaves and young animals are born.

effects on wildlife

At the South Pole, the Sun does not rise at all in winter, so it is very cold there.

Areas near the Equator have only small changes in day length. They stay hot all the time.

December
Nights are long and it is winter in the north. It is a hot summer in the south.

northern winter

southern summer

Climate connections

Climate change is shifting the seasons. The small increase in temperature is making springs earlier, summers longer and hotter, and winters shorter.

northern autumn

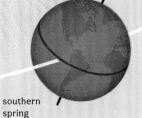

southern spring

September
The cool, damp weather of autumn arrives in the north. Spring comes to the south.

Autumn
Leaves change color and fall from the trees. There are fewer daylight hours, and nights get longer.

Land and sea
Seasons vary in different places. Land heats up fast in summer, but the ocean warms up slowly. In winter, the land cools down very fast, but the ocean keeps its heat.

Areas far from the sea often have the extremes of icy winters and very hot summers.

Places on the coast usually stay cooler in summer and do not freeze in winter.

Winter
Colder weather arrives, sometimes with snow and frost. Many trees lose all their leaves.

Climate zones

While weather is what happens every day, climate is a measure of how hot or cold, wet or dry an area is most of the time. The climate in each area, or zone, has a big effect on the types of animals and plants that live there. If the climate changes, this may introduce new challenges that the wildlife and plants cannot survive.

Tundra

Here, it is so cold that the ground is frozen solid all year round. Large plants cannot push their roots down into the frozen ground, so only small plants, such as moss, survive here.

A reindeer's fur has two layers for extra warmth.

Prairie grassland

In North America, the grasslands are called prairies. The same kind of zone is known as the pampas in South America and the steppes in Asia. These grasslands have very low rainfall, so no trees grow on them.

Bison herds graze on the grasslands.

MAP KEY

- Tundra
- Taiga
- Woodland
- Rain forest
- Savannah
- Desert
- Polar desert
- Prairie grassland

Sloths are perfectly built to live in tall trees with their long limbs and curved feet to grasp branches.

Penguins have lots of blubber (fat) under their skin to keep warm.

Rain forest

Close to the Equator, the weather is very warm and wet all year round. This allows tall, dense rain forests to grow. These are home to half the animals on Earth.

Polar desert

It is very cold in the frozen zones that surround the North and South Poles. It is also very dry, as there is not much rain, which is why they are called deserts.

Woodland
Many woodlands have trees that lose their leaves in autumn, then regrow them in spring. The trees shade plants and wildlife that live there.

Taiga
This zone includes the largest forests in the world. Taiga forests are filled with evergreen conifers, which are home to many different animals.

Thick, woolly coats protect mountain goats from the cold in the high mountains.

Climate connections
World temperatures rising quickly will affect all the climate zones. Polar areas will get smaller and the tundra will thaw. Animals and plants will not be able to cope and may disappear forever.

Mountains
Tall mountains can have more than one climate zone. There may be woodland or jungle at the bottom and snow at the top.

Equator

habitat loss

28

Savannah
These grassy plains have trees scattered across them. Savannahs are dry for much of the year, but get a lot of rain all at once during the wet season.

Camels can go for days without drinking water, so they can survive in the desert.

Desert
There is hardly any rainfall in hot desert zones. Without water, few plants can grow and there is very little food for animals. By day, deserts may be baking hot, but by night, they can be freezing cold.

Elephants use their trunks to dig for water, creating pools for other animals to drink from.

what is the greenhouse effect?

The greenhouse effect is a natural process that warms the Earth. It controls heat from the Sun and makes Earth a comfortable place to live. But people have upset the balance of gases in the air. Now the greenhouse effect is making the world warmer, and that is changing the climate.

greenhouse effect

The greenhouse effect works the same way as a greenhouse in a garden. The glass lets in sunlight that warms the air, and it traps that warmth inside. Earth's air, or atmosphere, does the same thing.

trapping heat

Without the greenhouse effect, Earth would be much colder than it is now. Our planet's temperature depends on the amount of certain gases in the air.

Earth's atmosphere

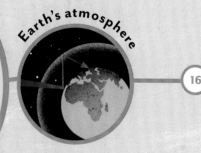

16

supporting life

The greenhouse effect makes sure that the temperature is just right for there to be liquid water in the oceans and rivers of Earth. No other planet in the Solar System has water on its surface.

water

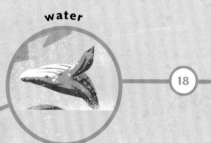

18

plants and animals

19

Earth's atmosphere

Our planet's atmosphere lets in energy from the Sun in the form of light, which warms Earth's surface. The natural greenhouse effect makes the atmosphere work like a blanket to trap the warmth and stop it escaping into space. But human activity is altering the balance of the greenhouse effect, and this is beginning to seriously affect Earth's climate.

Back into space
A small amount of energy rises from Earth's surface as invisible heat. This travels up through the atmosphere and back out into space.

Energy reflected by the atmosphere

Reflected energy
Some light is reflected back into space by gases and dust in the atmosphere. A smaller amount is reflected back by clouds.

Earth's atmosphere

Heat energy from the Sun

Invisible heat energy travelling back into space

Energy reflected by the clouds

Trapped energy
Greenhouse gases, water vapor and dust in the atmosphere hold onto some of the energy.

Greenhouse gases in the atmosphere

Energy trapped by greenhouse gases

Absorbed energy
The energy that reaches Earth is soaked up, or absorbed, by the surfaces of the land and water.

Light in, heat out
Light streaming from the Sun shines right through the air and hits Earth's surface. There, it heats the water or land. Then most of the energy leaves as invisible heat, which rises up into the air.

Thermosphere

The air here is very thin and it can get very cold at night. However, direct sunlight can make the top of this layer very hot.

satellite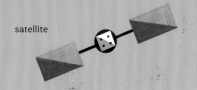

Layers in the atmosphere

The atmosphere is divided up into layers. The greenhouse effect warms the Earth's surface and the layer of the atmosphere nearest the surface. This is called the troposphere.

Mesosphere

This is the coldest part of the atmosphere. Gases in this layer stop meteors hitting Earth's surface. They cause the meteors to burn up.

meteor

rocket

comet

carbon increase

26

— 50 miles

— 30 miles

— 20 miles

— 6 miles

Gases in the air

Air is a mixture of several different gases. The three main ones, nitrogen, oxygen, and argon, have nothing to do with the greenhouse effect. Instead, tiny amounts of other gases act to trap the warmth that Earth needs.

Greenhouse gases in the atmosphere include carbon dioxide, methane, and water vapor.

nitrogen 79%

oxygen 20%

argon 0.9%

greenhouse gases 0.1%

Stratosphere

There is little water in this layer, so there are few clouds. Airplanes fly here to avoid storms.

Ozone layer

This stops most harmful ultraviolet rays hitting Earth.

Troposphere

We live in the troposphere. Here, water, dust, and gases mix to create weather.

airplane

Climate connections

Human activity is releasing more and more greenhouse gases. As a result, the amount of heat becoming trapped by the atmosphere is increasing and the world is warming up.

Water and life

Thanks to the greenhouse effect, Earth is a warm planet with a good supply of water. The temperature varies from place to place and changes from winter to summer. In most places, the temperature and the weather are just right for living things to survive. But climate change is altering this balance and putting all life on Earth at risk.

Extreme living

Even in the coldest places, most people can survive by wrapping up warm. However, there are some areas in the world where it is simply too hot to live.

The coldest place on Earth is Oymyakon, Russia. There, the temperature has reached as low as minus 130°F.

The hottest place on Earth is Dasht-e Lut in Iran. This reaches 160°F in summer. It is dangerous for people, so no one lives here.

effect on people

Life on Earth

Water is important because without it there would be no life on Earth. Liquid water is inside all living bodies on Earth, and all plants and animals must have water to stay alive.

Life on land
Animals and plants live in all but the very hottest and coldest areas. They all need water to survive.

Life in the oceans
The waters of our oceans teem with life. They also soak up the Sun's energy and carry it around the Earth.

Too cold

Without greenhouse gases warming up the atmosphere, the land would be covered in ice and the oceans mostly frozen over. The average temperatures on Earth would fall so much that scientists call this idea Snowball Earth. Life could exist in the oceans, but nothing would survive on land.

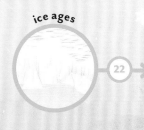

ice ages

22

Snowball Earth

Earth may have been frozen like this many hundreds of millions of years ago, before our atmosphere had completely developed. If it happened today, thick ice would cover the land, and the surface of the oceans would freeze over. There would only be a few patches of water near the Equator.

Too hot

Ours is not the only planet to have a greenhouse effect. Venus orbits closer to the hot Sun than Earth. Its atmosphere traps far more heat. It rains acid instead of water.

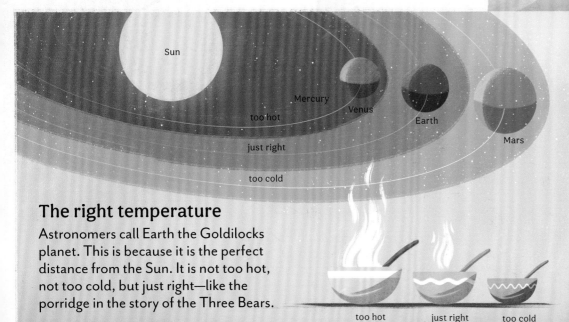

Sun

Mercury

Venus

Earth

too hot

just right

too cold

Mars

The right temperature

Astronomers call Earth the Goldilocks planet. This is because it is the perfect distance from the Sun. It is not too hot, not too cold, but just right—like the porridge in the story of the Three Bears.

too hot   just right   too cold

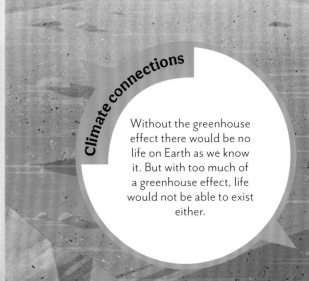

Climate connections

Without the greenhouse effect there would be no life on Earth as we know it. But with too much of a greenhouse effect, life would not be able to exist either.

what causes climate change?

The world's climate changes over time. It always has, and it always will. When it does this naturally, it is usually very gradual, and life on Earth can find ways to adjust to the new conditions. But today, human activity is making climate change happen much more quickly.

climate change

Climate is the pattern of weather conditions over a long period of time. Climate change is when there is a big difference in those patterns, such as temperature or rainfall, in a particular area.

natural causes

There are natural reasons for the climate to change slowly. It is important to understand the carbon cycle, ice ages, and the effect of volcanoes.

ice ages

volcanoes

the carbon cycle

human activity

People burn fuel to power factories and cars, and cut down forests to farm and build. These activities are leading to rapid climate change.

carbon increase

lost forests

farming problems

Ice ages

Over many thousands of years, Earth naturally switches from a warm climate to an ice age and back again. An ice age is the result of the lowering of global temperatures. This happens because Earth's orbit around the Sun changes shape so that sometimes it is closer to the Sun, and sometimes farther away. These variations cause major changes in the climate.

Woolly mammoths lived in the last great ice age.

Icy world
Long before people learned to farm food or build houses, the world was in the coldest part of Earth's latest ice age. A third of the planet was covered in ice sheets, some up to 1 mile thick.

snowball Earth

19

Pale planet
An ice age happens if global temperatures drop just a few degrees for a long time. When Earth's temperatures are lowered for years, the polar ice caps spread. Ice and snow reflect the Sun's rays, lowering the temperature more and making the ice age last longer.

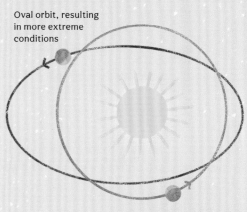

Oval orbit, resulting in more extreme conditions

More circular orbit, resulting in a steady climate

Moving around the Sun
When the Earth's orbit is nearly circular, the energy from the Sun is constant. When the orbit is oval, the energy causes greater changes in seasons and this affects global temperatures.

saber-toothed tigers

Climate connections
When less energy from the Sun reaches Earth, the global temperature drops. The climate changes dramatically and a new ice age begins.

Volcanoes

Volcanic eruptions throw out hot liquid rocks called lava. They also pour out clouds of ash and smoke, and greenhouse gases such as carbon dioxide. Clouds from a big volcanic eruption darken the skies, block out the Sun, and damage the ozone layer in the atmosphere. They can change the climate of the entire world for years.

Clouding the world

Volcanic eruptions change the climate by suddenly throwing dust and ash into the air. In large amounts, this pollution can spread all around the world. There are about 1,500 active volcanoes today, and the greenhouse gases they release make the world warmer.

Global dimming

Clouds from a volcanic eruption stop some sunshine reaching and warming the ground. This is known as global dimming. The dimming from a large volcanic eruption can change Earth's climate for several years.

controlling the climate
62

A Little Ice Age

Around 700 years ago, volcanic eruptions caused a drop in temperature of 3.5 degrees Fahrenheit in some parts of the world. It was unusually cold, and for a long time, many of the rivers were permanently frozen.

Climate connections

For relatively short amounts of time, volcanic dust can cause the planet to cool down. In the longer term, the release of greenhouse gases adds to global warming.

The carbon cycle

The greenhouse effect is caused mainly by carbon dioxide, which is made from carbon and oxygen. As well as in the air, carbon is in rocks, soil, and all living things. Living things use carbon to power their bodies. They release carbon dioxide into the air as part of a natural system called the carbon cycle. Any changes in the carbon cycle cause changes in the greenhouse effect.

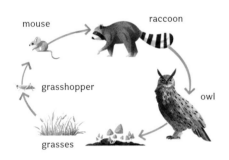

Food chain
All living things need energy to live and grow. Plants make their own food. The carbon chemicals made in plants move along the food chain as animals eat plants and each other.

Producing energy
Plants take carbon dioxide and water from the air. They use it to make food for themselves and animals.

Releasing energy
Plants and animals get energy from eating. Their cells take in oxygen from foods such as sugar. They also release small amounts of carbon dioxide at night.

Useful waste
Dead plants and animal droppings are eaten by fungi and bacteria, which turn this waste into soil. The soil then releases carbon into the air.

Earth's atmosphere

How carbon moves

In a well-balanced carbon cycle, the gas carbon dioxide moves from the atmosphere into living things, rocks, and soil. Animals and plants naturally release the gas back into the atmosphere.

Locked-in carbon

Some carbon chemicals get buried underground and become fossil fuels. Coal, oil, and gas (fossil fuels) are made from the remains of plants and animals that died millions of years ago.

Coal is formed from dead plants.

going wild

55

Using fossil fuels

Coal, oil, and gas give out a lot of heat when they burn. When they are burned to power factories and cars, carbon is released. It enters the atmosphere as carbon dioxide gas.

Oil and gas

The mixture of many hundreds of chemicals make oil, also known as petroleum. Oil is made from the remains of tiny sea creatures that formed a thick sludge on the seabed millions of years ago. The sludge also made smaller chemicals that bubble out as gases. People use oil and gas to power many things they use in everyday life.

Coal

Ancient tree trunks were gradually buried under many layers of rock that squashed them into coal.

Climate connections

By digging up and burning fossil fuels, people have upset the natural carbon cycle. Carbon dioxide is building up in the atmosphere more quickly than natural systems can soak it up.

Carbon increase

People are causing too many greenhouse gases to be released into the atmosphere. They do this by burning fossil fuels, in the way they farm animals and crops, and by the use of very powerful greenhouse gases such as nitrous oxide. All of this adds extra greenhouse gases to the air and upsets the balance of the natural carbon cycle. It causes the atmosphere to warm up and creates climate change.

Cement factory

We use a lot of concrete and cement to build our homes, cities, and roads. To make the cement and concrete for building works, fossil fuels are used to roast limestone. The limestone releases large amounts of carbon dioxide into the atmosphere as it breaks up.

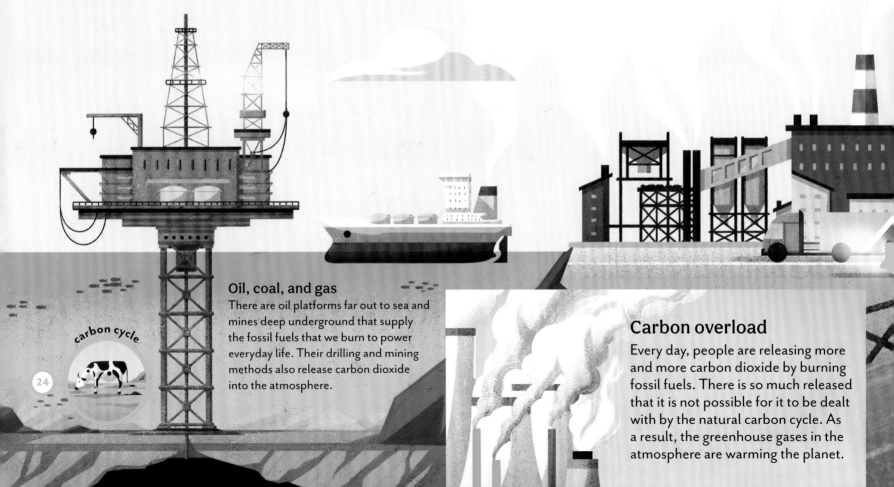

carbon cycle

24

Oil, coal, and gas

There are oil platforms far out to sea and mines deep underground that supply the fossil fuels that we burn to power everyday life. Their drilling and mining methods also release carbon dioxide into the atmosphere.

Carbon overload

Every day, people are releasing more and more carbon dioxide by burning fossil fuels. There is so much released that it is not possible for it to be dealt with by the natural carbon cycle. As a result, the greenhouse gases in the atmosphere are warming the planet.

Other greenhouse gases

Carbon dioxide is not the only greenhouse gas produced by people. We release greenhouse gases more powerful than carbon dioxide all the time by driving vehicles, using air-conditioning, raising animals to eat, and spraying fertilizers on crops.

greenhouse effect

15

carbon dioxide

other gases

Greenhouse gases

If a balloon was filled with the greenhouse gases we add to the air, about three-quarters would be carbon dioxide. The rest is made up of other, more powerful greenhouse gases. These gases are naturally removed from the atmosphere more quickly than carbon dioxide, but they have an even greater effect on climate change in the short term.

F-gases

Some gases contain fluorine—for example, F-gases—which are used in air-conditioning and medical inhalers. They are forty times more powerful than carbon dioxide.

Fertilizers

Nitrous oxide gas is released by the chemicals that are used to help crops grow faster. This gas is three hundred times more powerful than carbon dioxide!

Climate connections

When we burn fossil fuels, use fertilizers on our crops, breed animals to eat, and use F-gases, there is an increase in the greenhouse gases released into the atmosphere. This is causing the planet to heat up.

Farm animals

Animals are bred by us for meat, and there are billions of cows, sheep, and pigs farmed all over the world. The danger lies in the methane that is released when farm animals burp and produce gas. Methane is twenty-three times more powerful than carbon dioxide.

Lost forests

Forests help make Earth a healthy place to live. They take the greenhouse gas carbon dioxide from the air and store it in trees and plants. Forests also release life-giving oxygen and water vapor. If trees are cut down, carbon is suddenly released into the atmosphere. Today, on average, a forest area the size of a football field is cut down somewhere on Earth every second of every day.

Harmful release

When trees are cut down to clear the land, they are often burned. When wood burns, carbon dioxide is released into the air.

CO_2

CO_2 CO_2 CO_2

CO_2 CO_2 CO_2

Too much carbon

When a forest is cut down, the carbon dioxide it stores is suddenly released.

CO_2

CO_2

Soil erosion

Fewer trees mean less evaporation to make rain clouds. Soil becomes dry and crumbly and it is difficult for plants to grow.

Forest destruction

Forests are cut down to provide wood for fuel, as well as to clear land. The land is used to build towns, or to create farms for cattle or crops.

8

Life in the forests

Almost half of all the world's plant and animal species live in rain forests. Many are now in danger of losing their habitats. They cannot live anywhere else.

water cycle

Water vapor

Forests help control the world's water cycle. Trees release water vapor through their leaves in a process called transpiration. The steamy vapor travels up into the atmosphere, which is why rain forests get so much rain.

pure oxygen is released into the air

water and CO_2 combine in leaves

water travels from the soil

carbon dioxide

sunlight

Sunlight and plants

Plants combine carbon dioxide from the air with water from the soil to make their own sugary food. The energy needed to do this is collected from sunlight. This process is called photosynthesis. Pure oxygen is released into the atmosphere.

oxygen

Climate connections

People are releasing greenhouse gases by burning forests. This changes the atmosphere, boosts the greenhouse effect, and causes climate change.

Farming problems

All around the world, the way that people farm is having an effect on climate change. Modern farming methods are designed to make as much food as quickly as possible to feed everyone. But using chemical fertilzers and growing crops on the same patch of land every year mean that more and more greenhouse gases are released into the atmosphere.

Fertilizers
Most farmers add artificial chemicals called fertilizers to the soil to boost their crops. Without them, the world's farms would only produce two-thirds of the food we need. But these fertilizers create greenhouse gases and can kill off the bacteria and fungi that would naturally help the plants return carbon to the soil.

Destroying the carbon cycle
In the wild, the carbon cycle works well because it is balanced. Plants flourish in good soil with the right food. But when forests are cut down and land is used for the same crops again and again, carbon is released and the damaged soil cannot support new plant life.

Carbon in the soil
The soil contains four times as much carbon as is in the air and five times as much as is inside all the living things in the world. Many of the ways we grow crops release carbon from the disturbed soil. In the air, it becomes yet more of the greenhouse gas carbon dioxide.

going wild

54

Farming around the world

About a third of the land on Earth has been turned into farms and fields for growing food. The destruction of forests for farmland, and the increased use of farm machinery and fertilizers, have damaged soil and released carbon dioxide into the atmosphere.

Plants, or meat?

A field growing plants can feed many more people than the same area of land used to raising livestock (food animals). However, some places are too dry, too windy, or too rocky to grow crops, and animals are the best way to feed the local people.

livestock

fruit and vegetables

alternative foods

61

Failing crops

When the same crops are grown in the same place again and again, the soil loses all its nutrients and minerals. The land is then less suitable to grow more crops. It is better to farm different crops each year.

Climate connections

Many modern farming methods cause soil damage and release major greenhouse gases into the atmosphere. They put the carbon cycle out of balance and contribute massively to global warming and climate change.

Resting the land

It is important to find ways to stop farming contributing to climate change. One way is to allow a field to rest and let weeds grow. The farmer cuts down the weeds and plows them into the soil, where they will rot into useful chemicals.

what will
happen to
Earth?

Climate change is already making a difference to our planet. Average temperatures are increasing across the world. In the future, more ice will melt and sea levels will rise. There will be more extreme weather, which will result in more floods, droughts, and forest fires.

our planet

Every part of our planet will continue to be affected by climate change. Life in the sea and on the land cannot adapt fast enough if temperatures rise or fall dramatically. More extreme weather and sea level changes will cause damage.

extreme weather

Climate change brings fiercer storms, including hurricanes and floods. In other places, there will be drought and wildfires.

storms

drought

wildfires

oceans and seas

The atmosphere and ocean warming cause rising sea levels and changes to the way the currents flow. Carbon dioxide causes chemical changes in the ocean.

rising sea levels

currents

chemical changes

Changes in weather

Climate change causes more rain and stronger hurricanes. It also makes weather patterns stick around longer in the same place. When it keeps raining for days on end, there are more floods, and when the rain comes less often, there are more droughts. If we allow climate change to continue at such a fast rate, things will only get worse.

types of weather

8

More big thunderstorms

Thunderstorms are very dangerous and can cause lightning and tornadoes. Tornadoes travel fast over land and can knock down whole rows of houses. The strong storms that cause tornadoes to form will become more common with climate change.

Hurricane power

In the last twenty years, hurricanes have been increasingly powerful. Climate change warms sea surfaces and makes the wind speeds of storms much stronger. The resulting floods can devastate large areas of farmland and coastal cities.

Melting permafrost

In most of the Arctic, the ground is frozen all year round. It is called permafrost. As the climate warms, the permafrost has begun to melt, releasing huge amounts of the greenhouse gases.

Bubbles of methane released by melting permafrost

Droughts

Climate change alters the places that rain falls. This can bring drought to areas that previously have had enough rain. Drought threatens animal and plant life, and means that people cannot grow the crops they need to survive. In the worst cases, grasslands can become deserts.

Wildfires

Droughts make the land very dry, and forests and meadows can catch fire more easily. Wildfires are natural events, but longer droughts make the fires hotter and larger. This destroys more forests, kills wildlife, and threatens people's lives.

dangers for people 45 →

Droughts kill plants first. The soil is damaged by a lack of water, and the plants wither away after only a few weeks.

Most animals run away from a wildfire. Some hide underground and wait for the flames to pass. All of them lose their homes, and many do not survive.

climate zones 12

Climate connections

Climate change causes more extreme weather. If climate change continues, there will be fiercer hurricanes, stronger winds, larger floods, longer-lasting droughts, and more wildfires.

Rising sea levels

One of the big effects of climate change is that it causes sea levels to rise. The oceans are getting warmer and ice sheets are melting. When water heats up, it expands, taking up more room. The increase is already enough for low areas near the sea to get flooded more often, especially when there is a storm or hurricane. This will happen more often in the future.

Ice sheets
An ice sheet is a thick layer of ice that covers land. Fresh ice is added to the sheet far inland, and giant icebergs break off and melt where the sheet meets the sea. Climate change means the icebergs are forming faster than the fresh ice does, and the whole ice sheet could shrink and disappear. This would add huge amounts of extra water to the oceans.

Experts think that sea levels will rise by at least 1 foot by by the year 2100.

cold water travels from the cold polar regions

warm surface flow

cool subsurface flow

warm water flows from tropical areas

the water cycle

Expanding oceans
The water in Earth's oceans expands as it gets warmer, so it is gradually taking up more room and slowly rising higher up the shore. Melting ice from large sheets of ice on land, called glaciers, adds extra water to the sea, and that makes the sea level rise even more.

Current slowdown
Ocean currents flow all around the ocean, with warm water at the surface and cold water in the deep ocean. The currents are important for climate because they transport heat. When sea ice melts it slows down the ocean currents, cooling off certain places, especially Western Europe.

MAP KEY

 cool water

 warm water

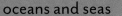

Changing the map

On an Earth without ice, the map of the world will look very different. The rising water will wash over today's coastlines and flood far inland. Some countries will get much smaller, islands will disappear, and many coastal cities will be underwater.

Melted ice sheets and warmer seawater are threatening to flood coastal cities.

As sea levels rise, the rivers and sea channels around New York City will grow much wider and deeper.

If all the ice melted

If the world's ice sheets melted completely, the sea level would rise by nearly 200 feet. That is the same height as 14 elephants standing on each other's backs! This will not happen for a few thousand years, but action is needed to stop it.

dangers to people

44

New York in danger

The city of New York is already surrounded by water. If nothing is done to stop climate change, the rising seas will turn downtown New York into a flooded, watery world.

Climate connections

As climate change warms seawater and melts ice sheets, sea levels will gradually rise. Low-lying islands and coastlines around the world will be flooded.

Changes to oceans

Climate change is causing as many problems in the oceans as it is on land. Seawater is a mixture of different things, including salt and the greenhouse gas carbon dioxide. Carbon dioxide combines with the seawater to make carbonic acid, the same stuff that gives fizzy drinks their fizz. Today, this extra acid is destroying sea creatures and habitats such as coral reefs.

Healthy reef

Corals are animals that live together in colonies. They are made colorful by the tiny algae that live inside them. A healthy coral reef teems with life. More than a quarter of all marine creatures live in and around these colorful habitats.

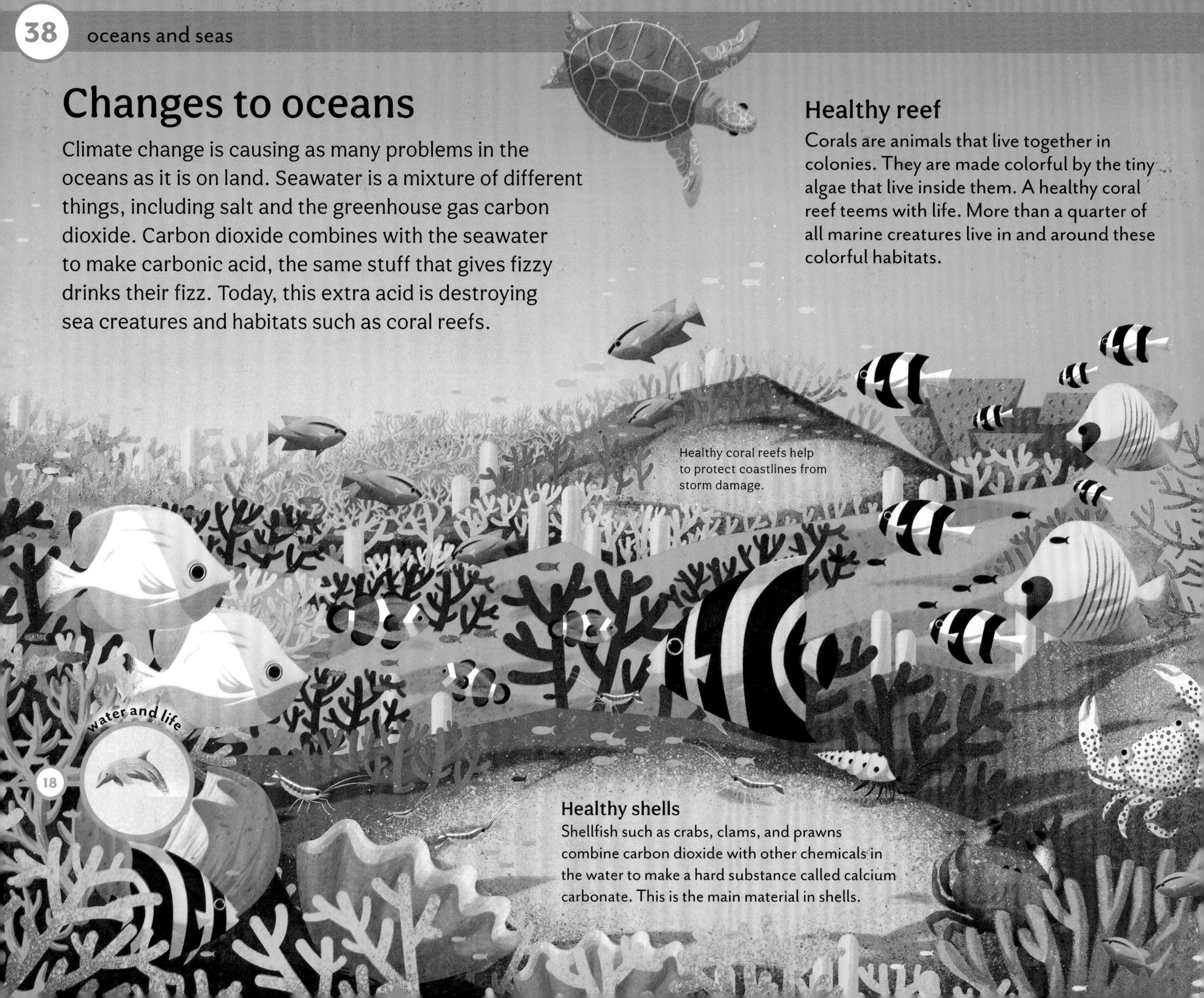

Healthy coral reefs help to protect coastlines from storm damage.

water and life

18

Healthy shells

Shellfish such as crabs, clams, and prawns combine carbon dioxide with other chemicals in the water to make a hard substance called calcium carbonate. This is the main material in shells.

Unhealthy reef

Extra acid in the seawater is making corals grow more slowly. When the water becomes too warm, the corals also lose the algae that give them their color. The corals go completely white. This is known as coral bleaching. It makes the coral weaker and it is more likely to die or become diseased.

About half of the world's coral has already died, and experts are not sure if it will ever grow back in the same place. All the animals that lived on these reefs have lost their homes.

Climate connections

Climate change is already causing global warming. If it continues, there may not be any coral reefs left in 20 years' time. We would lose most of the animals and plants that live there.

Unhealthy shells

Extra acid in the oceans from climate change is making shell-building more difficult. Shellfish such as crabs and prawns are making thinner shells than before.

what will happen to life on Earth?

All plants and animals on Earth live in their own areas, or habitats, on the planet. Climate change is causing the Earth to warm up very quickly. In the future, if we do not stop this from happening, the lives of most plants and animals will be harder and, in many cases, impossible.

life

Nine million different types of plants and animals live on our planet. If we do nothing, everything—from tiny bacteria to huge whales—is in danger from climate change.

wildlife

Animals and plants are under attack from climate change. Many are in danger of dying out altogether.

mass extinction

42

hotter climate

43

people

Climate change is already altering our lives. If we do not stop it, we may lose our homes to flooding or our crops to drought. We could also suffer from more diseases.

flooding

44

drought

45

tropical diseases

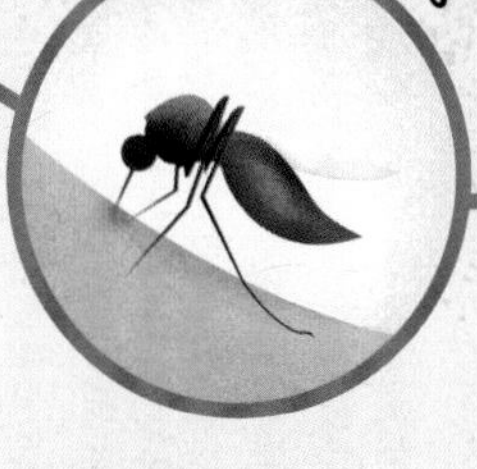

45

Effects on wildlife

Today's rapid climate change is making the world warmer and spreading new diseases. It is destroying habitats and harming wildlife. Animals and plants need more time to adapt gradually to change. If we do not quickly slow the rate of climate change, there will be a mass extinction of our animals and plants.

Melting ice

The North and South Poles are warming up faster than any other place on Earth. Melting ice is putting animals such as the polar bear at risk. Sea ice is where the bears hunt for seals.

sea ice

rising sea levels

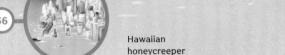

36

Hawaiian honeycreeper

New diseases

Small birds, called Hawaiian honeycreepers, are dying from a new disease. This was carried to Hawaii in the Pacific by mosquitoes. The mosquitoes are able to survive because climate change has made Hawaii warmer.

Extreme weather

Monarch butterflies travel on a long migration south to Mexico in winter. But climate change is causing worse storms than usual, and many of the butterflies do not survive the journey.

Mosquitoes live in warm climates.

Changes to the seasons

As our climate warms, plants are appearing earlier than normal in spring. They need flying insects such as bumblebees to help them make seeds. But it is too early in the year for many insects, which are still growing. There are increasingly fewer seeds and so fewer flowers.

Disappearing turtles

Sea turtles are in great danger from climate change. They lay their eggs on tropical beaches. Sea level rise and stronger storms are destroying these beaches. Also, the coral reefs where turtles find food are being damaged by the warmer waters.

Green turtles travel to tropical beaches to lay their eggs every two years.

Seeking water

Asian elephants have to travel farther each day to find the water they need to survive. Cimate change is making areas of the world hotter and water sources are drying up quickly.

Plant poisons

Monarch butterfly caterpillars feed on the poisonous leaves of the milkweed plant. Normally, the leaves do not harm them. A hotter climate is making the plants produce more poison. This is too much for the caterpillars, so they have no food.

milkweed

Asian elephants

Climate connections

Climate change is heating up our world. Life on Earth is finding it difficult to survive the changes. If the world continues to get warmer, many plants and animals will die out, or become extinct.

Dangers for people

People will not escape the effects of climate change. The world's biggest cities may have to be abandoned and people forced to move. Our supplies of food will be affected and, in some areas, there will not be enough to eat. Diseases that were once just a problem in a few remote places could soon spread around the world.

When cities are flooded, people have to be rescued by helicopters and boats.

extreme weather

34

Flooding

Rising sea levels and more frequent storms have a big effect on coastal areas. Powerful storm winds push surges of water up and over coastlines and into towns and cities, causing them to flood. The water flows away again, but it is dangerous and leaves a lot of damage.

Scientists predict that over the next 30 years, 400 million people will be looking for a new place to live.

Forced to move

It is not possible to live in badly flooded areas or places where it is too hot. People affected by climate change have to move to survive. More and more, people will need to travel over continents to find areas with the space to build new towns and cities.

Spreading disease

Diseases such as malaria, yellow fever and the West Nile virus kill many people. They are spread by mosquitoes and other biting insects that live in warm climates. With global warming, the insects will spread into more places, carrying the diseases with them.

Too much heat

Droughts have been drier and lasted longer in recent years because of climate change. These events are dangerous for people. There is not enough rain, and the shortage of water leads to crops failing, so there is not enough to eat. When it is too hot for too long, plants cannot survive.

High heat destroys plants and makes the land unfit for food crops.

Spoiled farmland

As the world heats up, life will change for people in many countries. With more floods and droughts, farmland will no longer be fit to grow food. People will have to learn to eat and grow different foods.

Climate connections

People need places to live where they can find shelter and grow food. Big floods and temperature rises caused by climate change will force more and more people to move to find new homes.

alternative foods

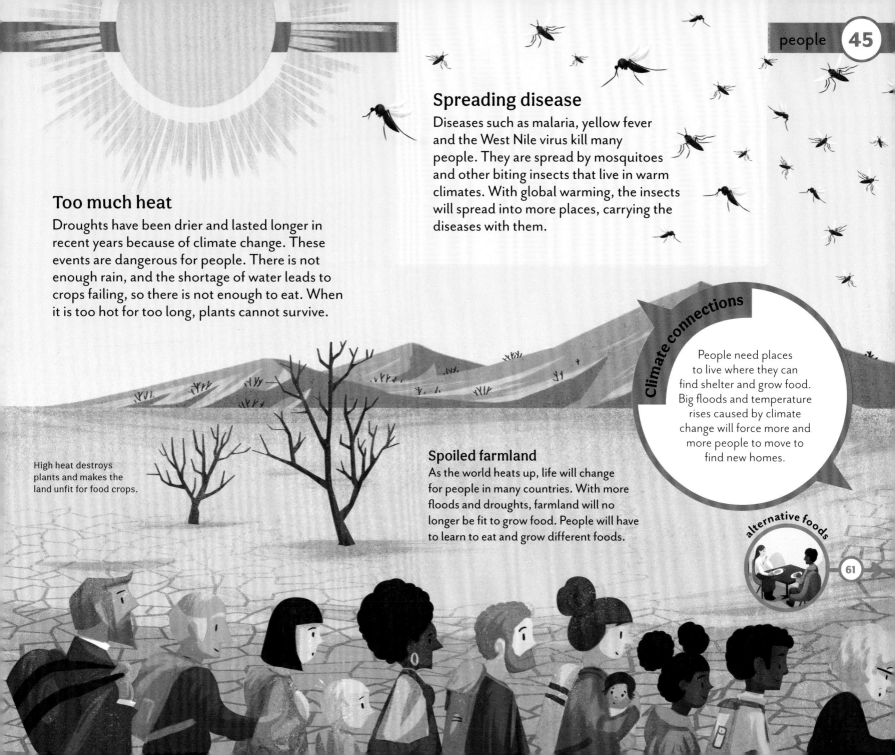

61

can we
stop climate
change?

There are lots of things that we can do to stop climate change. Many of our activities are powered by oil, gas, and coal. These fossil fuels release harmful greenhouse gases that trap heat. We need to save energy, find alternative sources of energy, and prevent waste.

stop it!

Stopping climate change means doing things differently. We need to use less of the world's precious resources, and reuse and recycle more. Everyone must work together to solve climate change.

carbon footprint

Everyone has a carbon footprint. It measures greenhouse gases produced by everyday activities. There are ways of reducing it.

energy use

48

reduce, reuse, recycle

50

renewable energy

Wind, water, and sunshine can be used to produce renewable energy. This is energy that does not pollute the air or the water.

wind and water

52

heat and light

53

going wild

By planting new forests, we can remove greenhouse gases from the air. Letting nature "go wild" can also help to slow down climate change.

reforesting

54

rewilding

55

Energy use

Every year, the activities of all the people in the world produce nearly twice as much carbon dioxide as Earth's carbon cycle can process. That extra gas in the atmosphere contributes to global warming, which leads to climate change. But some people have a much larger carbon footprint than others. How big is yours?

What is a carbon footprint?

A carbon footprint is a measure of how much carbon dioxide and other greenhouse gases are produced by your everyday activities. This includes what you buy, how you travel, and what you eat. Just like real footprints, every carbon footprint leaves its mark on the planet—and it contributes to climate change.

Bad heat

Fossil fuels such as gas and oil are burned to make the heat that keeps our houses warm.

Half of the amount of greenhouse gases we produce comes from power plants and how we heat buildings.

carbon increase

26

Bad waste

When garbage ends up in dumps or landfills, it creates the dangerous greenhouse gases methane and carbon dioxide.

Bad fuels

Vehicles powered by fuels, such as gas and diesel, have a high carbon footprint. They release a lot of carbon dioxide into the atmosphere.

Reducing your carbon footprint

Your carbon footprint is not fixed. On the opposite page, you can see some of the things that cause climate change. On this page, you can see everyday things that can be changed to reduce your carbon footprint.

Green energy

Instead of burning fossil fuels, we can power homes and cars with electricity made from renewable energy. This can shrink everyone's carbon footprint.

renewable energy   52

solar energy

wind power

Green waste

Cut back on waste by using less and for longer. Recycle what you can to cut down on greenhouse gas emissions.

Climate connections

Every person, community, company, and government can reduce their carbon footprint by changing the way they act every day. It is important that everyone takes responsibility for climate change.

Green travel

Use public transport and electric cars to reduce your carbon footprint. Better still, get around by walking or cycling.

Recharging station for electric cars

Reduce, reuse, recycle

To combat climate change, we all need to be less wasteful and use less energy. We should think carefully about whether we need something before we buy it. Then we should reuse items as much as we can. When we have finished with things, we should find ways to recycle them that use the least amount of energy.

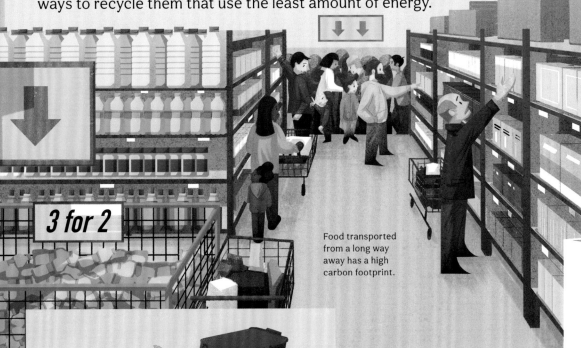

Buying new things before old ones are worn out creates unnecessary pollution and more carbon emissions.

3 for 2

Food transported from a long way away has a high carbon footprint.

Buying new
Most of an object's carbon footprint comes from the process of making it. The manufacture of new items such as mobile phones and computers uses rare materials and large amounts of energy.

Food waste
It is estimated that today, one-third of all the food produced in the world goes to waste. Leftover food can be used to fight climate change. Instead of just being thrown away, the food can be composted to make biofuels that can be used instead of fossil fuels.

High carbon footprint
When you shop in a supermarket, you need to think about the carbon footprint of every item. Should you be buying a new item in packaging that is then thrown away? Are you replacing something that still works?

It is too easy to throw away anything we have finished with. But too much ends up being burned or in landfill. Many things can be recycled.

TECH REPAIR STATION

Often, replacing one component is enough to make a broken phone or computer work again.

Don't throw it away

When something breaks, try to fix it, or ask someone else to help. Do this before throwing it away and getting something new or, ideally, nearly new.

battery recycling

Batteries and soda cans are very easy to recycle, and save a huge amount of greenhouse gas emissions.

Lower carbon footprint

You can help fight climate change by choosing where to shop. Ask shopkeepers whether they use a lot of packaging, if the food they sell is local, and what they do about recycling waste.

Many shops allow customers to buy loose fruit and vegetables.

If you need to buy something that is packaged, try to choose recycled materials.

Reuse and recycle

Ask shopkeepers if you can use your own shopping bags or containers. Reusing these over and over again reduces carbon emissions and does not add to waste pollution.

what can you do?

69

Food that is grown locally and in season has a much lower carbon footprint.

Climate connections

A good way to reduce your carbon footprint is to throw away less. Instead, buy only what you need, reuse it when you can, and recycle when it is completely worn out.

Wind, water, heat, and light

The Sun is always shining somewhere, the winds blow, and the rivers flow down to the sea. These sources of energy are constantly replaced or renewed with a fresh supply. We need to harness this renewable energy to help us to stop climate change and prevent waste. We can use renewable energy instead of burning fossil fuels like coal, oil, and gas.

Biomass energy

Wood and other plants can be used as a solid fuel or turned into gases that can be burned. Although carbon dioxide is released, the plants absorbed the gas when they were growing. So the two things balance each other out—they are almost carbon-neutral.

carbon increase

26

Hydroelectricity

This is electricity made by the movement of water, most often by a dam built across a river. Renewable energy like this can be used to produce the electricity that we need for our everyday lives.

A balancing act

Renewable energy can help to stop climate change, but it can cause other problems. For example, making the concrete to build dams releases a lot of carbon dioxide into the atmosphere. On the other hand, hydroelectric power does not produce any carbon dioxide emissions.

Solar energy

The Sun's energy supports all life. It is possible to collect some of that energy and turn it into electricity by using solar panels. The electricity can then be used to power everything in the home.

Solar panels can be fixed onto roofs, cars, boats, and satellites.

Wind farms can be built on land or offshore in shallow seas near the coast.

Wind power

A wind turbine is a tall tower with blades that are made to spin by the wind. The spinning motion powers a machine that makes electricity. Winds affect every part of Earth, and many wind farms are built on top of hills to catch the strongest winds.

new energy sources 58

Geothermal power

The word "geothermal" means "Earth heat." Deep inside our planet, there is hot, liquid rock. Close to hot springs and volcanic craters, the heat is near enough to the surface for us to use.

Climate connections

Power from water, wind, and sunlight will not run out. This is energy that does not give off greenhouse gases and so will not contribute to climate change.

Reforesting and rewilding

It is important to repair the damage people have done to natural environments. Forests, swamps, wetlands, and other habitats play an important role in the fight against climate change by locking in carbon. But these wild places can only exist if we protect them. We need to reverse damage and restore the natural balance, allowing animal and plant life to thrive.

28

lost forests

great white egret

Forests

Trees protect the planet against climate change by absorbing carbon from the atmosphere. Large areas of forest have been destroyed for farms and logging. We need to protect older forests and plant new ones.

Mangrove swamps

Protected mangrove swamps and tidal salt marshes store a huge amount of carbon. They also shelter coastlines from storms, acting as a barrier and preventing flooding.

Wild animals

Wolves and other wild animals play a part in keeping the climate in check. Wolves hunt deer that eat young tree shoots, helping forests to grow.

Achieving a balance

Over time, people have released too many greenhouse gases into the atmosphere by their activities. They have changed the natural balance for wildlife and plants all over the world. In order to prevent climate change, that balance must be restored. This can be done in part by looking after and rewilding natural forests and wetlands.

Wetlands are a combination of wet and dry areas.

Wetlands

These areas, rich in wildlife, absorb carbon from the air. Also, when the wetland plants die, they do not break down and release their carbon into the atmosphere. Instead, the carbon gets buried in the mud and is locked away.

Climate connections

Nature can help to solve climate change. If we protect and rewild forests, oceans, and wetlands, they will help to reduce the amount of carbon dioxide in the Earth's atmosphere.

Nature helping itself

Many animals look after the balance of their own habitats. When beavers build dams, this helps to slow down the rivers, creating new ponds and wetlands. By doing this, the beavers help more plants grow, and these, in turn, store carbon.

changes to oceans

36

Trawling the seabed

When ships trawl for food, their fishing nets stir up the seabed. This destroys the ocean floor and releases carbon that is stored there into the water. It is better for the environment to fish with a rod and a line, and it is important not to overfish.

Inside a bog

A bog is a wetland where peat builds up. Peat is a kind of thick, hard soil formed from dead grass and leaves. It takes hundreds of years to form and it locks away carbon absorbed from the air.

can technology solve it?

Technology can help us to reduce climate change. There are lots of new developments in clean energy, carbon-free transport, and carbon capture. But to have any effect, we need to make the right choices about the way that we live, use energy, and travel about.

clean technology

Scientists are finding new ways to make and store energy. These will change the way we live and travel so that we do not release so many greenhouse gases.

new energy sources

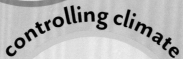

58

smart technology

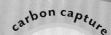

60

technology

Researchers are looking at ways to tackle climate change. They are using science, technology, and engineering to find clean energy that does not damage the Earth. Some are even exploring the idea of living on another planet!

controlling climate

Trees and plants remove extra carbon from the environment naturally. Geo-engineers are looking for artificial ways to do this.

carbon capture

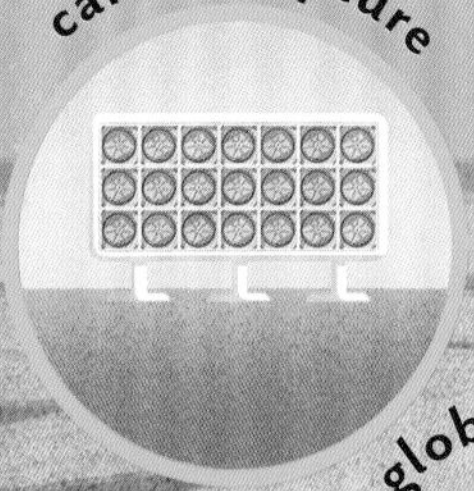

62

global dimming

62

a new home

Some people think that life on our planet will not survive climate change and we'll eventually need a new place to live.

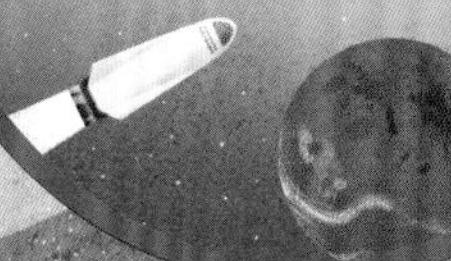

living on Mars

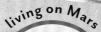

64

renewable energy 52

New energy sources

We are already taking some energy from the power of the wind and the sunlight and converting it into electricity. It is important now to develop this clean technology so that it happens on a larger scale at less cost. Sometimes we make more electricity than we need, and we must work out ways to store it safely until it is wanted. Scientists are also looking for alternative sources of energy, including experiments with clothing and algae.

The bigger the waves, the more power we can get, so future power systems will need to be strong enough to survive fierce storms.

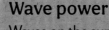

Wave-power generators work by being pushed up and down by the waves rolling past them.

Smart clothing of the future

One day you might be able to make a supply of electricity to charge your mobile phone just by moving around. Smart clothing made of special materials could collect the energy from your arms and legs. The materials would give out electric currents as they are stretched and twisted by your movements.

Wave power

Waves on the surface of the ocean are made mostly by the wind. Scientists are experimenting with generators that could collect this wave power. It is a really difficult thing to do, but technology might make it work.

Tidal power

Twice a day, the seas rise up our shores to make high tide and then go back down again for low tide. This huge daily movement of water is a powerful source of renewable energy. We just need to use it!

Nature's power

Plants, algae, and some bacteria convert light from the Sun into sugar in a process called photosynthesis. Scientists are trying to copy the natural photosynthesis system to use sunlight to make oil or other fuels instead of sugar.

sunlight and plants 29

Tidal lagoons can have artificial islands.

Climate connections

We use some renewable energy already. But we need to use more renewables and less fossil fuels to slow down climate change. Time, money, and government support are needed, and time is running out.

River barrages

A tidal dam, or barrage, can catch energy at the mouth of an estuary. As the tide flows in and out, it rushes through water turbines and generators that convert the energy into electricity.

Tidal lagoons

It is possible to capture energy from tidal lagoons. A natural lagoon is a seaside lake that is filled up by the tide like a giant rock pool. An artificial lagoon is built especially to catch tidal energy. The flow of water in and out of the lagoon can be used to make electricity.

A tidal barrage is a two-way dam where a river meets the sea.

Smart technology

As well as living greener, we need to live smarter. Smart technologies that make better use of our supplies of energy are available already. In the near future, all houses and cars could be run on cleaner energy, with renewable energy taken from solar panels and wind turbines instead of oil and gas. Cars can be electric, not run on nonrenewable gas or diesel. People can hold meetings online instead of jetting around the world to talk to someone.

solar panels

Automatic blinds go up and down to control temperature.

Smart meters control the amount of water and electricity used so there is no waste.

electric vehicle being charged

Smart robots connect us with people all over the world so we travel less.

A big rechargeable battery stores unused electricity.

your carbon footprint

48

Transport

As well as switching from gas to electric, it is important not to build too many new cars. In manufacturing, greenhouse gases are released. Car sharing could be the answer.

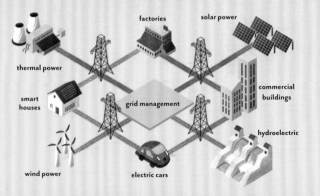

thermal power

factories

solar power

smart houses

grid management

commercial buildings

hydroelectric

wind power

electric cars

Smart grids

Today, all our electricity comes from a few big power plants. In the future, it is likely to come from wind turbines, solar panels, and storage sites all over the place. Artificial intelligence will be used to control the supply network.

Storing electricity

There is a new technology that allows us to store spare electricity as liquid air. Electric pumps can be used to squeeze and squash air until it turns into a liquid.

This house makes its own renewable electricity using solar panels. It sends any extra power to its neighbors.

Cleaner travel

In the future, journeys could be by Hyperloop. It looks like a train but moves as fast as a jet plane. It will have fewer carbon emissions and be less polluting than today's cars, trains, and planes.

A smart house of the future

If new technology is used in our homes, it could make a big difference. Solar panels and wind turbines can store power. Smart lighting and appliances can switch themselves off to save energy and control temperature.

Meals are prepared with food grown in a way that causes less climate change.

what can we all do? 68

GM crops   non-GM crops

Climate connections

We need to alter the way we live and the things we use if we are to slow or stop climate change. Smart technology can help us to do this if we use it properly.

Low-carbon food

A lot of the food that we eat has a high carbon footprint. In the future, we need to think of alternatives. Insects are low-carbon foods. They are easy to keep, and grow very fast. Insects can even eat animal droppings and turn them into healthy food.

Changing farming methods

Farmers have been selecting the best versions of crops for as long as there have been farms. Now, by using genetically modified, or GM, crops, they can select even better options. GM crops will cut fuel and fertilizer use and can grow in conditions, such as drought, in which other plants could not survive.

Controlling the climate

Today, some scientists are looking for ways to stop climate change happening so quickly. They are investigating different ways to cool the Earth. These include carbon capture to reduce the amount of carbon in the atmosphere, and global dimming to stop some sunlight reaching the Earth's surface. Many of their ideas are just theories at the moment, and will not work until new technology has been developed.

volcanoes 23

Cooling the Earth

When the amount of sunlight reaching our planet is reduced, the Earth's surface cools down, like when a large volcano erupts. This is called global dimming. Dust pumped into the atmosphere from aircraft would reduce temperatures all around the world. It would also turn the sky white and cause major changes to our water cycle.

Some engineers are hoping that captured carbon can be turned into a fuel.

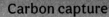

greenhouse effect 15

Carbon capture

A carbon-capture system is able to pull carbon dioxide out of the air. This can help to stop the greenhouse effect and prevent global warming. Scientists have worked out how to do this, but are trying to develop the technology that will let them do it on a very large scale.

Carbon storage

If large amounts of carbon dioxide gas can be been captured, it will need to be stored safely so that it does not cause climate problems in the future. One idea is to pump it down old, empty oil wells.

Nature's answer

Trees pull the greenhouse gas carbon dioxide from the atmosphere and store it for long periods. By planting new trees, and looking after existing forests, everyone can help to stop the rise in temperatures around the world. Scientists are working on ways to make trees that grow faster and store more carbon.

A brighter Earth

If Earth could be made paler and brighter, then it would reflect back more of the Sun's heat and light and reduce the greenhouse effect. One way to do this is to add silver iodide dust to the air. This would increase the number and brightness of clouds swirling around our planet and reflect more of the sunlight.

Reflecting sunlight

Paler ocean waters reflect more of the Sun's heat, cooling the Earth. Scientists think that ships could pump jets of air into the surface waters. The tiny bubbles left would make the water paler, and reflect more sunlight.

Algae and carbon

Scientists have found that when sea algae die, they sink to the bottom of the ocean, carrying carbon with them. If we could add nutrients to the ocean, more algae would grow and more carbon carried to the seafloor. But the nutrients would also sink, so we would need to continuously add more to the ocean surface.

Climate connections

Scientists are researching some clever ideas, but the solutions are not ready yet, and there might be unexpected effects. More money and time is needed to develop technology to help us to stop climate change.

Can we move planet?

Climate change is damaging so much of the natural Earth that some people think it might be better to set up home on a different planet. The only planet that scientists have thought about so far is Mars, but there are many problems with living there. When people eventually make the long journey, they will land on a planet that does not have air to breathe, water to drink, or food to eat. They will have to build their own shelters. It would be far better to stop climate change on Earth and make it a perfect home.

Flight to Mars
It is difficult to reach Mars, which is more than 150 times farther away from Earth than the Moon. It takes at least nine months for a spaceship to travel there, and so far, only robot explorers have made the journey.

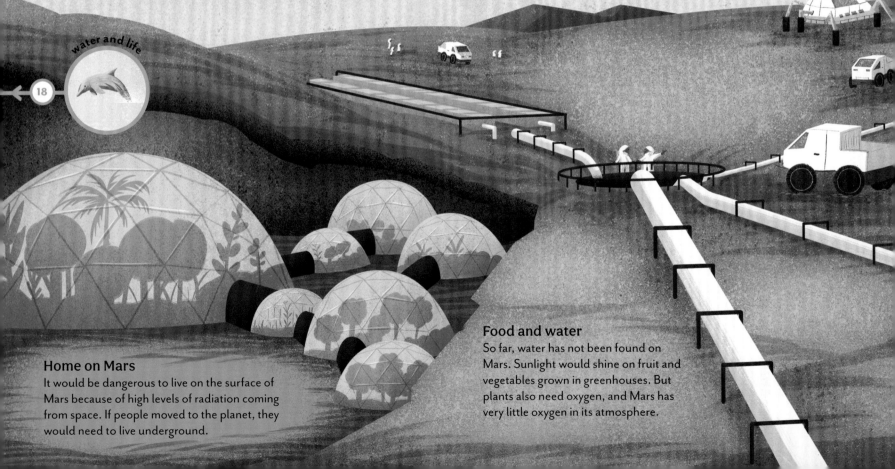

water and life

18

Home on Mars
It would be dangerous to live on the surface of Mars because of high levels of radiation coming from space. If people moved to the planet, they would need to live underground.

Food and water
So far, water has not been found on Mars. Sunlight would shine on fruit and vegetables grown in greenhouses. But plants also need oxygen, and Mars has very little oxygen in its atmosphere.

Life on Mars

It is very cold on Mars. In summer it can sometimes get to just above freezing. In winter it is much colder than Earth's polar regions. Everyone's home on Mars would have to be airtight because there is no breathable air, and all materials would have to be brought from Earth on spaceships.

The spacecraft would need to have enough room to carry all the fuel for landing on Mars, and food, water, and air for the crew.

1. Dead algae creates living soil.

2. Algae turns Mars green.

3. Mars becomes warm enough for liquid water to form.

Terraforming

Biologists think that it might be possible in the future to turn a dead planet like Mars into a new version of Earth with algae and bacteria. Even if this idea worked, we do not yet have the technology to make it possible.

Mars is less sunny than Earth, but solar power would still work.

Small nuclear power plants could be brought from Earth to make electricity.

Fuel and power

There is no fuel or power on Mars itself. Although energy could be captured from the Sun, solar power would not be enough on its own. The astronauts would have to make their own fuel and power with materials brought from Earth.

Air to breathe

The Martian air is made up mostly of carbon dioxide, and any human would not survive more than 15 seconds. A spacesuit would need to be worn at all times.

Climate connections

The new technology needed to live on Mars would be much easier to apply to the Earth. We need to find ways to stop climate change, adapt, and stay on our own planet.

what do
we do
next?

Climate change is a threat to every one of us. We need to take action to stop it before it is too late. All of us—from world leaders and large companies to every single person—can make a difference. We need to work together to save our home planet and the life that lives here.

next steps

Governments from all over the world need to agree on next steps, then make rules in their own countries. Each one of us has an important part to play too.

working together

Climate scientists are investigating climate change and working to find solutions. All governments need to listen to their advice and take action.

climate science

68

governments

68

world agreements

68

every single person

You and your family can make a difference by thinking about the things you do every day. Your choices will change what big companies make and what shops sell.

travel

69

carbon footprint

69

food

69

What can we all do?

All around the world, people are learning about climate change and starting to take action. Many countries are getting together to make the big decisions that can make a difference. It is vital that governments and world leaders focus on renewable energy, rewilding, and alternative transport before time runs out.

Renewable energy
Making electricity with renewable energy means we will burn fewer fossil fuels. Far less fossil fuel means less greenhouse gas.

Rewilding
Planting huge new forests around the world will help to reduce greenhouse gases in the air.

Transport
Developing cleaner ways of making our journeys is a big part of the fight against climate change.

World meetings
World leaders need to get together regularly to agree on what every country can do. They must agree on rules for big companies to work in a way that will not cause climate change.

Research and technology
Climate scientists across the world are working together to understand climate change better. They can help the world's leaders decide on the best actions to take.

What can you do?

You can make simple choices in your everyday life that will help to prevent a climate disaster. Think about your own carbon footprint—what you eat, how you travel, what you buy, and what you wear. Reduce, reuse, and recycle, and make your voice heard as much as possible. Get involved in your community and make a difference!

Getting around

Avoid traveling by car or airplane whenever possible. Try to walk and bike for short trips and use public transportation for longer ones.

If you have some space for it, plant a tree!

At home

Reduce how you use energy at home. In winter, use less central heating and wear warmer clothes. In the summer, close the blinds or use a fan. Wash your clothes in cool water and do not use a tumble dryer.

Climate connections

Everyone in the world must take whatever steps they can to stop climate change. The actions taken by every single person are as vital as decisions by world leaders in this important fight to preserve our planet.

Food

Buy food that is grown nearby so it does not have to travel. Reduce how much meat you eat and eat more veggies.

Clothes

Mend old clothes and buy fewer new ones. Recycle clothes that do not fit anymore by giving them to thrift stores. It can be fun, as well as eco-friendly, to buy second-hand clothes too.

Spread the word

Help others to reduce their carbon footprint. One way to do that is to explain the problems clearly and make sure everyone you know hears your voice.

We can STOP climate change!

Let's work together!

Glossary

air pressure The weight of the air, which pushes down from above all the time.

algae Small plantlike living things that capture energy from sunlight and turn it into sugary food.

atmosphere The layers of gases and clouds that surround the Earth.

bacteria Tiny living things made of a single cell. Most bacteria cannot be seen without a microscope.

biofuel A fuel made from plant or animal waste as well as some farmed crops, such as corn.

carbon cycle The way that carbon atoms continually travel from the atmosphere to living things, into the Earth, and back again.

carbon dioxide A gas in the air that plants use to make food and that all plants breathe out. It is also released by burning fossil fuels. Too much carbon dioxide in the atmosphere contributes to climate change.

carbon emissions The release of carbon dioxide into the Earth's atmosphere.

carbon footprint The measurement of how much carbon dioxide a person's activities produces.

carbon-neutral Describes any activity that releases the same amount of carbon dioxide as it absorbs.

climate The typical kinds of weather that a place gets over time.

climate zone Areas of Earth that have the same kinds of climates. Deserts make one climate zone, while rain forests make another.

condensation The change from a gas into a liquid, caused by cooling.

coral bleaching When corals lose their bright colors and go white, often due to climate change.

current A strong movement of water through the ocean or a lake.

erosion The wearing away of the Earth's surface by water, wind, or ice.

evaporation The change from a liquid into a gas, caused by heating.

extinction The dying out forever of a type of animal or plant.

fertilizer A chemical that helps plants to grow faster and bigger.

food chain A series of living things that depend on one another for food. For example, a plant is eaten by a plant-eating animal that in turn is eaten by a meat-eating animal.

fossil fuel An energy-containing fuel, such as coal, oil, or gas, that is formed from the remains of prehistoric plants or animals.

geothermal Describes the energy produced by using the heat from inside the Earth.

glacier A huge mass of ice that flows like a river, but extremely slowly, down to the sea.

global dimming The way that dust and soot in the air blocks out the light and heat of the Sun, making the Earth slightly cooler.

global warming The warming of Earth's atmosphere, caused by carbon dioxide and other greenhouse gases trapping heat in the atmosphere.

greenhouse effect The way that certain gases in the atmosphere stop heat from the Sun from escaping back into space, warming up the Earth.

greenhouse gases Gases in the Earth's atmosphere, especially carbon dioxide, that play a part in the greenhouse effect.

habitat The place where an animal or plant usually lives or grows.

hydroelectricity The electricity that is made by capturing the movement of water.

ice ages Especially cold periods in the Earth's history when ice spread over most of the planet.

ice caps Thick layers of ice and snow that cover the North and South Poles.

ice sheet A layer of ice that covers the land.

iceberg A large piece of ice floating out at sea.

landfill A place where people bury their garbage in the ground.

livestock Farm animals that are raised for food.

molecule A group of atoms linked together; everything is made of molecules.

orbit The path that an object in space takes around a planet, a moon, or a star.

oxygen A gas in the air needed by most animals to survive.

ozone layer A thin layer of gas in the upper atmosphere that absorbs harmful radiation from the Sun.

permafrost Soil that is always frozen, even in the middle of the summer.

photosynthesis The way in which plants use the energy in sunlight to turn carbon dioxide and water into sugary food. Oxygen is released during photosynthesis.

pollution Any substance that harms living things by poisoning the air, land, or water.

power plant A place where electricity is made.

recycle To change waste into new, usable material.

reforestation The planting of trees in places where forests have been cut down.

renewable energy Energy that can be made from a source that will be naturally replaced, such as wind, water, or sunshine.

rewilding The reintroduction of wild, natural habitats where farming, mining, and other activities have destroyed them.

smart technology Modern machinery and methods that collect data and use artificial intelligence to carry out tasks.

solar panel A device, often on a roof, that uses solar cells to make electricity from sunlight.

water cycle The continuous journey that water makes from the sea to the sky, onto the land, and back to the sea.

water vapor Water in the form of a gas.

weather The conditions in the air right now at a certain place on Earth.

wildfire An uncontrollable fire that sweeps through forests and across fields, burning everything in its path.

wind farm A set of wind turbines that make electricity from the flow of the wind.

wind turbine A modern windmill that makes electricity as it spins in the wind.

Index

Author: Tom Jackson
Illustrator: Dragan Kordić
Consultant: Dr. Marianna Linz, Harvard University

Editor: Miranda Smith
Designer: Lee-May Lim

EARTH AWARE
K I D S

Copyright © EarthAware Kids, 2021

Published by EarthAware Kids
Created by Weldon Owen Children's Books
A subsidiary of Insight International, LP.
PO Box 3088
San Rafael, CA 94912
www.insighteditions.com

Weldon Owen Children's Books
Assistant Editor: Pandita Geary
Art Director: Stuart Smith
Publisher: Sue Grabham

Insight Editions
Publisher: Raoul Goff

ISBN: 987-1-68188-559-9
Manufactured, printed and assembled in Turkey
First printing 2021 ELM/06/21